CADASTRE

ROBERT BRINGHURST

CADASTRE

ROBERT BRINGHURST

Kanchenjunga Press
Bloomington, Indiana

Certain of these poems have previously appeared or been scheduled for publication in the following periodicals:

 Concerning Poetry
 Contemporary Literature in Translation
 Quarry
 Stoney Lonesome

The drawings reproduced on pages 35 and 49, and the drawing of Ποσειδῶν χαλκεοθώραξ reproduced on page 9, are the work of Patrick Morrison. The originals are currently in the collection of the artist.

The drawing reproduced on page 65 is the work of Paco Castillo.

THE CONTENTS

I

II

III

I V

4

...διδόναι γὰρ αὐτὰ δίκην καὶ τίσιν ἀλλήλοις τῆς ἀδικίας κατὰ τὴν τοῦ χρόνου τάξιν, ποιητικωτέροις οὕτως ὀνόμασιν αὐτὰ λέγων.

"...for they must pay one another the penalty and compensation for their mutual injustice in the order of time," as he describes it in these rather poetical terms.

Simplicius, *Physics*,
quoting Anaximander

HERAKLEITOS

I

Herakleitos says a dry soul is wisest and best.
Herakleitos is undeniably
right in these matters. These
bright tatters of wisdom, cast
over grey welter and spume should at any rate yield
a few visions and reflections, a little light
cutting crosswise like a fin,
splayed against the sea's grain
or annealed on the wave crest.

A dry soul. Dry: that is to say
kiln-dried, cured like good lumber or old Bordeaux,
salt-pork and pemmican, meat of the soul
under the chokecherry,
                            sunlight
and sea-salt arrayed in the grain.

II

Herakleitos says something of concord—not
like a carpenter's clamp or lashed
logs, as in Homer.
Harmony with an arched back,
laminated ash upended like an unlaid keel, the curl
of live flesh in the fire, flexed
like the soul between muscle and bone, like
the bow, like the lyre.

III

All things are exchangeable for
fire and fire for all things,
like gold for goods and goods for gold,
or so sings old
                    Herakleitos.

IV

Herakleitos says something which cannot be put
into prose, though the Bishop Hippolytus quotes
it as though it were prose.   Its essence is this:

mortal immortals are immortal mortals,
the breath of the one is the death of the other,
the dying of one is the life of the other:

mortals are deathless, the deathless are mortal,
living in the body the death of the other,
dying into air, earth and fire, siring

the other, the utter
incarnation.

V

Wind stirs his ashes.

SONG OF THE SUMMIT

The difference is nothing you can see —only
the dressed edge of the air
over those stones, and the air goes

deeper into the lung, like a long fang,
clean as magnesium. Breathing
always hollows out a basin,

leaving nothing in the blood
except an empty
cup, usable for drinking

anything the mind finds —bitter
light or bright darkness or the cold
corner of immeasurable distance.

This is what remains: the pitted blood
out looking for the vein,
tasting of the tempered tooth and the vanished flame.

STUDY FOR AN ECUMENICAL WINDOW

Moses and Mohammed knew
the long hollow in the silence through
the script in the star-eaten stone
and the incessant alternation
of the new-honed
light and the rust-pocked, chipped, uneven
edges of the sun. They saw beyond
the carbon at the heart of it, diamond
and damascene steel, the crystal
riveted into the bone
that has been
cut to fit the socket of the hand.

They looked through oxide and scale,
oak-bark, hide, nail, the enamel
over the live nerve. Yes, certainly, they knew
the taste of marrow,
visions that grow in the bone, things seen
in the sap before it is frozen,
in the hard unclouded fluid.
Moses and Mohammed
saw the blood before the air eats
into its essence, when the light sits
not quite on it but
about it, without weight.

Moses and Mohammed, yes
they saw the surface
that is deeper than the water,
listened to the light
and the undertow's sound.
They knew the word will congeal around
the heart and in that instant will be
brighter than at any time later,
tighter than the crystal, finer
than the blade that has been sharpened
into effervescence,
ground down an atom at a time.

They saw inside the iridescence,
listening to the clinkstone cut
the wind, and watching the water shut
the white light out and into colors.
Underneath, they knew the blood's
similar
surface in the darkness
of the artery, the darkness
gathered in against it, not
quite on it but about it,
fluctuating, humming under
the pulse in the incessant

alternation, the insistent
oxidation under the iced-over
heaps of decayed leaves and abandoned
timber: a darkness that is
razor-like and ragged, like

the stone of the circumcision,
the die's edge, the final incursion
of the chisel, the precise place
where the sculpture grows
out of its base. Flint for the light to strike,
backdrop for the diamond's
museum-case.

POEM ABOUT CRYSTAL

Look at it, stare
into the crystal because
it will tell you, not
the future, no, but
the quality of crystal,
clarity's nature,
teach you the stricture
of uncut, utterly
uncluttered light.

STROPHE FROM SOPHOCLES

(cf. Heidegger, *Einführung in die Metaphysik* IV,3)

Strangeness is frequent enough but nothing
is stranger than man —
thus
and across
the grey-maned water,
heavy weather on the southwest quarter,
moves amid sea-thunder,
tacking through the bruise-blue waves.
And he rubs at the earth,
the eternal, the tireless
eldest of goddesses,
driving the plough in its circle year after year
with the offspring of horses.

FOUR GLYPHS

I

Tláloc's jacket was sleeveless
and made out of cloud.
A string of green stones
sank into his shoulders.
The tall blue sky was his brain.

Tláloc planted the rain.
He planted it loud
as boulders
and quiet as butterflies' bones.
And in a time to come he will reap it.

II

The wind is the feather of the lizard that the lizard
never wears,
             and the cloak of the kidnapped king,
the rain's roadsweeper, and the wind
is the god in his ocelot anklets:
                          the wind
leaps out of the mountain, wind with white teeth
and bright talons, light and dark wind within wind,
air in the air's heart and arteries, dark
wind in the vein under live tissue of wind,

bones made out of bright air and the dark air
swollen around them, tendon and flexed
muscle of wind, air like white onyx set in sockets
of the wind and the light on them, stopped light,

caught the way the sunlight slides over garnet
or cabochon sapphire:
                    wind
pounces out of the mountain, the wind
leaps out of the overturned shield.

III

The hummingbird's tongue
under the sun's black anther,
fire taking the sky's measure,
light's core soaring over
blue air, wave, rock and water,
over eagle-cactus, pine,
and the spiked dust of the summer highlands,

bright blade of blue sunlight
over the stone,
spalled off the solid block
of the sky's light like a smoke-thin
razor of obsidian
or an unseen wing.

IV

Tezcatlipóca at Tula, the Toltec
Smoking Mirror, can be looked for in four
directions:

Red in the East, the fertile light, the flayed
bright water in the canebrake, quivering
flesh of the air alive over the limber reed.

Black in the North, the vanished absolute
fruit of the fire, the cold flint flat between
two hands, tasting of death and the dead land.

White in the West, where the wind lies
over gold water and under a beam
like flame on a flat stone, under hewed timber.

Blue to the South, under the sun's beak, where
the rabbit hears the iridescent bird.

KERRY SHAWN KEYS

"*tu ne cede malis sed contra audentior ito*"
(Aeneid VI, 95)

He spoke of Tithonos, who withered into a bedridden voice
East of the world, behind panels of pale light
       that slide shut in the silence.

"Tithonos," he said, "and this business of Big Daddy Zeus
fucking over Tithonos...and Eos lonely...no lover
       for four thousand years..."

and then something, luminous alloy, electrum of air
overtaking his eye and the thought formed, "armed with the story,
       I will be wiser."

THE THIRD GENERATION: A TREATISE ON THE GODS

*(Pluralitas non est ponenda
sine necessitate.* —Ockham*)*

I

Apollo, full sunlight, the sky's depth, distance, the god,
the vision when the bark falls
back as from a casting, leaving
light taking form from the mold.
The musician, Apollo
of clear-eyed cognition, the song's clear intention
and accuracy, word after word,
tone after tone, the tuned string ringing
true, silent as bowshot.
Proportion not in mixture but in order of relation
of shapes in continuum, order of portions
distinct in one medium, moving and still,
patron of mathematicians, physicians,
the luminous law without word, the will only
toward clarity and clarity of form,
the sun's brightness
and lightness of breath like a scalpel, the will
moving weightless, unobstructed by the texture
or density, cleavage or grain
of the material.

II

Artemis, alpine, keeper of quail,
of geese on the long migration, guardian
of birds, beasts, and the young
of humankind,
a glimmer at the edges of the mind,
goddess in the high clear meadow and the high clear air,
and in the clarity of flow
below the hillside spring.
Unforgiving,
unloving, but bringer of ease
to women in the time of menstruation and the time
of bearing children.
The archeress, dancer, the rider
of unbridled stallion and stag, the flight of the teal
over the next hill and always
past the last mark of the plough,
the iced light over alders, light's tread on meadowgrass,
lunar ore in the air. The tremor over
the unclimbed peak, starlight in darkness,
over the dark root of the cypress a grainless unharvestable
timber of the clarity of crystal.

. . . .

The light leaps
like an arrow past the air.
Ridiculous to ask
what god, what goddess;
the light keeps
the arrow's character.

III

Athena, the mist off the sea, the translucence
clinging in the cedars and the olive trees,
morning, the mind, the clear light cut
as with a razor, taking count of the color
and the light's own form.
Mistress of horses, goddess of clear-sighted skill,
of technical fluency, manual facility,
the working edge of the soul.
The clean cut of the shipwright, the potter's glaze,
the navigator's knowledge and the measurement inherent
in the glance, and in the lucid gaze.
And in the gray light of measured day one sees
farther than in full sunlight, sees detail, motion
and features in full relief; Athena
is absence of error,
mallet and chisel making visible the mandatory form
at will's intersection with material.

•   •   •   •   •   •   •

Slightly more slowly
light inside the air leaps, keeps
the air's own character,
reaps every latent image in the air,
oak into amber, the form cut
clean, taking count of the grain,
it is the Mycenaean spear.

IV

Hermes, the god in the windfall, god of good luck
and of bad, clandestine, uncanny, companion
of perjurors, burglars and thieves,
                                    the shape-changer,
claim-jumper, odd god, guide into the darkness, guide
out of darkness into half light at his leisure.
Purveyor of dreams and of all things achieved but
unasked for, distraction, surprise, sudden
silence in speech.

.   .   .   .

Aphrodite, scythe out of sea-froth, the sea-spun
cloth, the web of the unmuscled water over
basalt jaws, like a gull on the sea-god's shoulder.

Blood surface dusted with light, the sleek gleam of flame,
neither molten gold's meniscus nor the harsh, clear
color of unworked silver, nor the cedar's grain.

Superfluity, superficiality,
ancillary grace become the fundamental
motion, the flowing action of an empty hand.

.   .   .   .

Ares, the coral foam
on the colorless lip

the quaking the suction the sudden
absence of suction,
retrieving the blade from the belly

the quaking and the bright bright colors how they fade
the fresh bowels lying in the dirt and light

shattered bone in the blood, the thud
of big guns taking place of the earth's pulse,
darkness sucked in,
darkness sucked up as if sustenance,
viscous, sucked in.

Men of Rome, finding Ares untutored,
in the Iliad a coward, uncivil, short of glory,
transferred light from the image of Phoebus Apollo to Mars
pro patria mori,

darkness made to flow in the vein
as if under harness.

V

Apollo song's spirit,
Athena the soul,
but the impulse
is Artemis.
Ridiculous
to ask who has
the clearest eyes.

THE GREENLAND STONE

Gods immersed in the masked
North American air
vanish like cryolite,
vanish like the kayak's
white stone anchor hitting
bright blue arctic water.

The snowfall in the stone
clears when the lightfall slows
the way the heart's thought, the eye's
mossy chalcedony
and the mind's wet marrow
clarify when it quickens.

A PORTRAIT

I gave her a metal leaf once.
It was curled a bit, enough to hold
two pearls, like unfused water drops, but
adequately simple.
Gold, in fact. Tin
wouldn't have done, because,
even though I didn't really care
about the substance,
what I wanted was
that one, sure meditative color...

It was...well, despite the pearls, it was
really, now that I think of it, just
a high-class cardboard cutout
of a candle-flame, I guess...though...yes,
yes, I guess it was.
I meant, however, as I say, only
to give her a metal leaf—that is
a piece of metal anyone would take to be at least
the reminiscence of a leaf.
Identifiable, clear-cut,
a kind of metal memory
of a leaf...and evidently I...

    the same and not the same
    a noun in the elusive sense
    a verb in the elusive tense
    the same and not the same

Of course I meant
it to be permanent...

     that will not fit the pages of a book
     respond to water or decay
     with winter
              and won't blow away
     whether I look or do not look

Well, shit. It'll fit the ground
like any other kind of leaf.
It'll turn back to a nugget
like the unmined ore...

     never quite eroding into nowhere
     whether
     buried or unburied
              never
     quite caught up and carried

But I should have made the bastard out of
cardboard, instead of...

     south to nowhere
     like the image
     in its passage past the mirror

getting this thing that gleams

like one of those goddamned candle-flames...

    without a mouth to capture
    or articulate its message

It would have been safer!

FOUR LOVE POEMS FROM VIDYAKARA'S ANTHOLOGY

1

Fireflies inlaid
in cloth of darkness; lightning flash;
storm of a size I can guess at
from the thunder; elephant's call;
scent of first ketaki blossoms
open on the east wind; falling rain.
No knowing how a man will stand
these nights, a long way from his love.

2

Because it cannot bear
comparison to my long-eyed lover's face
the moon continues to recast
itself in a dark place far from here.

3 (Rajashekhara)

The blossom swells in the bud, the leaves
still hide inside the sprout, the note
in the cuckoo's throat
anticipated now but not yet heard.
If Love lays hold of his bow now, just two days
of practice will do; he'll win the world.

4 (Rajashekhara: Poem Against the Classic Sanskrit Similes)

Where her face is seen, no mention is made of the moon.
Against her skin, the gold grows wan.
If a man's eye meet with hers, his thought is not of waterlilies.
Seeing her smile, first pressing of moonlight seems stale.
Her brow draws back like Love's bow—though more beautiful.
...But of course, it is well known,
the god would not have thought her
                                        with tautologies.

LULLABY FOR BRENDAN

Wind is the world's voice but there are
very many singers, many
songs, many singers, and the
great still wind that is the
sky has many winds within it
moving, moving many ways.

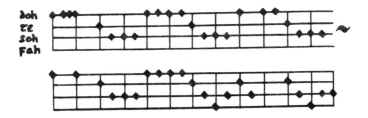

ANTISTROPHE FROM LEOPARDI

for Michael Peglau

This hill has been standing in my heart a long time,
thick with brush that cuts off much of the horizon.
I sit here, I look out and I think about things —
about long spaces beyond this place, and silence
that is superhuman; about the deep quiet
that happens sometimes in the heart and that almost
replaces the pulse.
                    Whenever there is wind here
I compare its pronunciation of the leaves
to all that silence. And whenever I do that
I think of eternity and the centuries
of the dead as if here living with the present
and the wind's sound. Then my thought drowns, but I find it
sweet, like sweet water, going down in that great sea.

LE DEBAT DU CUER ET DU CORPS DE FRANÇOYS VILLON

Qu'est ce que j'oy? Ce suis je. Qui? Ton cuer...

What's that noise?
        It's me.
It's who?
        Your heart,
        suspended, flayed
        on a frayed thread.
        Strength, substance, lifeblood
        gone
        when I see you so —
        lonely, withdrawn,
        in the corner like a cowered dog.
Why's that?
        Your carefree ways.
What's it to you?
        It cuts me deep.
Shove off! Give me some peace.
        What for?
I'll think it over.
        Will you? When?
When my childhood ends.
        I'll say no more.
I'll manage.

43

What's your plan?
To be an honest man.
    You are, incidentally,
    already thirty.
Merely a mule's age.
    Still the childhood stage?
No, daddy.
    So. I see
    stupidity has solid hold.
Where? On my collar?
    You understand
    nothing.
Yes I do. I'm in command
of flies in cream.
It seems to me
one's white, the other's black. There's that
distinction.
    Is that all?
What do you want? Textual
explication?
If I haven't said enough by now,
I can say it again.
    Then you're done for.
I'll resist.
    I'll say no more.
I'll manage.

    Sure, sure, it's me who mourns,
    but you're
    the one who suffers

and the one who's harmed.
If you were
just another moron, we might find
some illusion of excuse.
But you don't give a good goddamn.
You don't distinguish
between beautiful and lethal.
Either your head is hard as a pebble,
or you hold that this
misfortune is better than honor.
What's your answer
to my argument?
Just that I'll be above it when I die.
God, what consolation!
What sage eloquence!
I'll say no more.
I'll manage.

How did this malignancy begin?
With my malignant luck.
When Saturn packed
my satchel, he tossed in
these little problems.
That's ridiculous!
You're master of these things
and behave like a slave.
See what Solomon wrote in his scroll:
"A wise man," he says,
"has power over planets,
strength beyond the planetary pull."
I don't believe it. I am and I will be

however they have made me.
      What did you say?
Yes, by God.   That's what I believe.
      I'll say no more.
I'll manage.

      Don't you want to live?
I pray for the strength to do so.
      Then you have to. . .
What?
      Follow your conscience. Read
      unceasingly.
Read what?
      Read metaphysics.
      Stay away from fools.
I'll see to it.
      Now don't forget.
I'll tie your words like string
around my finger.
      Don't procrastinate. Don't wait
      for further damage.
      Now I'll say no more.
I'll manage.

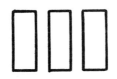

THE POET, HAVING AT LAST ENCOUNTERED
THE MUSE

Lord, this lady is the worst
of many I've met who've ladled thirst
like milkmaids out of the buckets of their eyes
and tried to make me drink it down.

I'll rhyme her ass until it's pursed
and puckered like a mouth that's nursed
a cactus into a flower twice her size
and wear that blossom like a crown.

O may her belly bloat and burst
and her progeny all be ugly, cursed
with critics, bibliographers and flies.

A DOCUMENT

Under the overweight, parachute-shaped
deciduous signet, Mr Smith's
glossy ink gaped.

"We thank you
for your interest in
the Chestnut Tree Review
and for allowing us to read
that which, herewith,
we return to you.

"After careful consideration
we have decided
that it does not
    meet the needs of
the Chestnut Tree Review."

With careful desideration
one is guided,
so subtly, to
"meet the needs of"
the Chestnut Tree Review.

POEM OF THE SEXTON'S TINNITUS

"What a world of solemn thought their monody
compels!" (Poe)

I open the shut
box for a perfectly
            obvious purpose.
The box resembles a mummy-case
rather
        than a coffin.
Ah.   There is further
communication
            from under the Chestnut.

"Nothing here,"
says the editor's letter,
                "rings the bell from you."

Can it be true?
I? I guilty
            of unresonant matter?
Ah.   But this
is a resonant clue
            to eventual success.

One tires,
of course, after three

thousand years,
                of the harping and song
of Demodokos
and the lutany
                of scholars under Kung.
These instruments are
dated,
            and Pound has discussed them completely.
Naturally,
they are therefore
unstrung
            and electroplated.

And one can be called
"connected" only
                when properly installed
adjacent one or more
                    forms of the electrified ding-dong.

Europe, mauled
and refinanced, dissolves
                        in the glory of celestial
    cuckoos and glockenspiels,
toasting with phylloxera-resistent
                        ox-blood and scuppernong.
Hammer of breath in new bugles
and sousaphones
                and insistent
gabble and groans
of elves

in the rust-proof barns
      underlie the orchestral
  big deals
    and boondoggles.

One turns,
as a matter
of course, to the clatter
      of aphorism,
to musical
belles
lettres and political
    gongorism.

But "nothing here,"
says the editor's letter,
     "rings the bell from you."

Ah. Now therefore
I too
know the ultimate metaphor.
I know my purpose and my place.
I know that the appalling blue
dolphin-torn sea,
the wind in the wet coral,
arcs of the gulls,
and all
the antiphonal
formulae of grace
fall

cleanly into formation
                    on deck at eight bells
and like land-locked white old
admirals
          are harmoniously tolled
to transcendence and memorial
fruition
          under the carillon.

THREE WAYS OF LOOKING FOR THE NORTHWEST PASSAGE IN THE SHIPYARDS OF BRISTOL AND ROUEN

I: The Poet as Chef de Cuisine

Polyarchitectonical metamellifluphors
soothe the savage beast
for hours or years with the strange taste
of marled multitudinous flavors.

Polyetceteras also may nourish him —
may that is, if he is able to digest them.
But they lie, often, to say the very least,
loose, on reaching the lower intestine.

This, perhaps, is their purpose.
In the end, their apparent constitution
indicates intentional
purgation of the corpus.

II: Exemplum: The Poet as Chickenfarmer

I

The sun comes up.
It is round!

II

Some cows walk past me,
Moaning like repentent fascists.

III

Windmills turn slowly overhead.
The !

III : Encounter: The Poet as Volcano

He preaches wildness, less control,
eruptions from volcanoes of the soul
like molten bone.

A lavaflow the mouth could mold
would harden like ancient bubble gum
and we could trace the toothprints...

I roll cool agate and onyx on my tongue
to mirror the flavors that are already on it.

WORDS TO BE SUNG INTO A PIECE OF PAPER AT
216 BEACON STREET

> *"I the poet William Yeats*
> *With old mill-boards and sea-green slates..."*

I the poet Robert Lee
Bringhurst, with used mahogany
I was given and broken marble I found
in the dooryard when I levelled the ground,

with used nails and borrowed tools,
a bent square and two half-illegible rules,
but nothing precut with one side sticky
rebuilt this cellar for my lover Miki,

and I don't give a damn if these words remain
when this fine old house lays open to the rain,
but I wish by god that great songs and old cities
had a higher place in life than dumb-ass ditties.

THREE EPIGRAMS

"Beauty is the marking-time,...the feigned ecstasy of an arrested impulse unable to reach its natural end."
(Hulme, or quoted by him)

1

This accidental folding of the hands —
archetypical
style, just as it stands

   That grace go
with my motion when I move

2

A sumptuous ass,
yes, and a candycane curve
to the high hard little tit, but
let it pass.

3 (*i.e.*: Marking Time in Stiff Meter)

"A carriage of high
nobility"—otherwise known
as:
"She walked
like
somebody'd stuck
a broomstick up her ass."

THE RHYTHMS OF IRENE

> *"She's got Elgin movements from her head*
> *down to her toes.*
> *She breaks in on a dollar most anywhere she*
> *goes."*

(Robert Johnson)

The rhythm method of controlled birth
of beauty in language means what Irene
thought it meant in another regard.

"The rhythm method?" asked Irene,
"I always thought that what that meant was
doing it. . . you know. . . that is. . . to music."

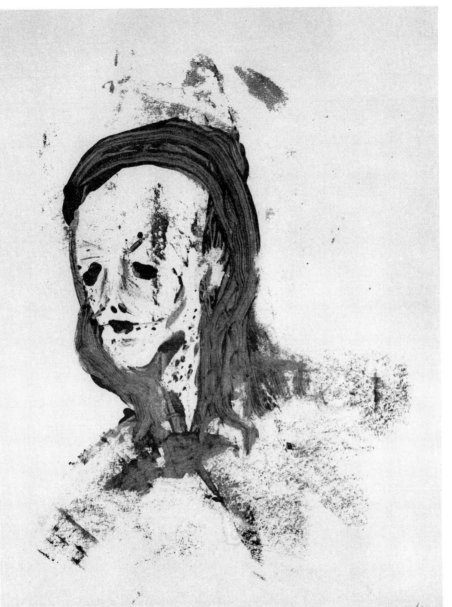

THE SONG OF MACUILXOCHITZIN

(Tenochtitlan, circa 1476; from the Nahuatl)

I raise my songs high,
I, Five-Flower,
gladden the god our father with my songs.
Start the dance!

Wherever,
however it is...do the songs go
up to the house of the god?
Or do your flowers only
grow on the ground?
Start the dance!

The Matlatzinca are yours,
my lord Itzcohuátzin.
And you, Axayácatl,
took Tlacotépec.
Over that city your flowers
and butterflies hovered.
This is great joy.
The Matlatzinca are there
in Tolúca, and in Tlacotépec.

Patiently he offered
flowers and feathers
up to the god our father.

He put the shields of eagles
in the arms of men,
in the war's hearth,
in the center of the field.
Like our songs,
like our flowers,
you, soldier with the shaved head,
gladden our father the god.

The eagleflowers linger
in your hands,
Axayácatl.
All of our allies
are decorated and drunk
with the warflowers,
the sanctified flowers.

The warflowers open
over our heads
in Ehcatépec, in Mexico.
All of our allies
are drunk with these flowers.

The princes have demonstrated their bravery,
all the Acolhuácan princes,
you, the Tepanécas.
Everywhere he went
Axayácatl's army won battles —
Matlatzinco, Malinalco,
Ocuillan, Tequalóya, Xochotítlan.

Now he returns.
In Xiquipílco
he was hit—speared in the leg by an Otomi
soldier named Tlílatl.

And Tlílatl went to the women
and said to them,
"You be the brave ones.
Fix up a splint and a bandage and go to him."
He lay there shouting,
"Bring me the Otomi
who gave me this legwound."
And the Otomi was scared,
and he said,
"They'll kill me for sure."
And he brought a gigantic piece of worked wood
and the skin of a deer
and expressed an immense reverence
for Axayácatl.
And his women are here now,
begging,
pleading with Axayácatl.

THE ODE OF IMR EL-QAIS

from the Arabic (circa AD 530)

Rein up
     and we weep here, mourn
a house, a girl—
          where the cornice
of that sand reef curls
between Miqrat and Toodih, Haumal and Dakhool.
North wind, south
              wind interweave; wind
mutilates the traces.
Stag dung is spattered like peppercorns
where the yards and cisterns were.
They loaded up one dawn
by these acacias.
            It was
like biting a colocynth.

Tending their mounts, my companions
are saying:
     Don't die grieving. Find
     some seemly end.
I cry again. Tears cure.
No solace here.
Not even enough ruin
left to lean on.

You were just this way with the woman before her,
Huwairith's mother. Also with her neighbor
in Masal, Omm el-Rabâb...

Perfume stirred around them when they stirred,
like odor of clove on a fresh east breeze,
and tears flowed over my throat as free
as blood, and soaked my scabbard.

You've had your share
of good days with the women.
That day at Dara Juljul
for example, couldn't be equalled.

Or the day I slaughtered my mare
for a gaggle of girls
and passed out presents from the saddle pack.
The girls tossed the fresh-cut camel flesh
high into the air.
                    I cut the suet
into tassles like twilled silk...

Or the day I climbed into Onaiza's howdah!
She yelled:
        Go to hell! Do you
        mean to make me walk?
The canopy kept swaying
with the two of us, and Onaiza was saying:
        Imr el-Qais, you'll cripple my camel! Get DOWN!
And then I said to her:

Give him the quirt, and let the reins hang.
Don't hold me off, you sweet little melon.
Why, I've come like this
even to pregnant women.
Even to a nursing mother!
(And diverted her, my dear, from her amulet-laden
little yearling.
Whenever he'd whimper behind her she'd hardly
half turn to him. Her other
half stayed under me.)

And one day, back of a dune,
a girl made excuses, swore her honor, and I said to her:
Easy, lady. Less of your coquetry.
Even if it's dead set
that you're through with me, be decent to me.
Dazzled you, maybe, this battle
between me and my love of you?
Dazed you that whatever order
you issue, my heart obeys?
Or is it that you think
I have disreputable habits? Then
by all means pile my shirt apart
from yours. These tears have only
one intent: they're meant to strike
with your bright barbed eyes
into the carnage of my heart.

And the prize yolk in the boudoir's shell,
whose tent no man at all

dares even to gaze on—
I've sported with her, totally at leisure.
I've threaded through the garrison that guarded her, eager
every man of them to kill me.
Pleiades lay
              like studs in the sky's folds.
She'd piled all but the last of her clothes,
as for sleep,
              by the curtain when I came.
And she whispered when she saw me:
        I'll be damned. You are
        disarming, I must say.
        And what if...I were also to find you
        rather charming?
I led her outside
and she trailed behind her
her finest skirt, dragged the dirt with it,
covered our spoor.
We crossed all the encampment, walked on,
found a soft little hollow in the crusted, wind-whipped sand.
I took her curls in my hand.
She hovered over me...

Slender the flanks, tender the ankles,
shapely the belly, taut, white,
not a gram
              of unfirm flesh.
Shoulders burnished like a silver mirror.
Whiteness, where whiteness
first blends into amber,

nourished on the whey of unstirred water.
She turns, there appears
a polished cheek.
She wards me away with the shy eye
of a doe with foal, as in Wajra.
Throat like the throat of a lithe white addax.
Neck not ungainly, no matter how she cocks it.
Not a flaw.
Hair down her back like a black cascade,
                              color of coal.
Luminous curls clustered like dates on the palm,
strands twined upward into
                    ravelled and unravelled braid.
And a waist as supple as my bridle rein.
Thighs like moist, pliant reed.

Motes of musk
brood over her bed in the sun's ray;
she sleeps until noon.

She gives, it is with tenderness.
Caterpillar fingers
like the wooly-worms of Zhabi;
no taint whatever of coarseness;
softly;
probing and gentle
as dental tools of ishil wood.

Goes out at evening, she glows there,
illuminates the gloom like an anchorite's light.

Pubescent boy or gone dreamer would stare
with full-blooded fervour at her

                                    standing there
half woman and half girl.

          Men's blindnesses distract them
          from their youthful inclinations.
          My heart is not distracted, knows
          no consolations,
          no diversion from loving you.
          Many have meant to argue against you;
          I've restrained them. I remember,
          my sincerity's won out
          against their censure.

But a night veiled like a breaking wave
broke over me, strewed every variety
of miserable luck in my way.
And I shouted to the night, when its loins stretched over me
and buttock-wash behind me heaved against me:
          Give birth to the dawn!
          What morning, even if you mothered it,
          could look like you?
          You bitch of a night,
          your stars are roped to stones!

I've lugged my kinsmen's waterskin,
laid it over my shoulder-blades

humbly and humped it
down a valley bleak as a wild ass's belly.
Lone jackal wailed
like an exile thinking of his kids.
I answered back:
      Jackal, we've had equal luck.
      Both clean out of money—
      if you ever had any.
      Or if either of us ever
      had anything, it's vanished.
      Whoever farms my acreage
      or yours, goes pretty skinny.

And I've left at first light, birds in their nests,
on a short-haired stallion, sired wild, huge,
attacking, backing, banking, outflanking
all at once—a boulder
                barrelled off the mountain on an avalanche.
Blood's hue simmers in his gray.
The saddle-felt sails
              straight off his back
like a pebble intercepted by a cataract.
He surges to second wind,
thunder under the sea-surge
                of his heartbeat,
like a kettle at full boil.
He flows, while the floating mares
falter and go stringhalt.
The light young jockey blows
            right off his back;

he whips the clothes
                    clean off the hard-eyed heavy rider.
He spins like a boy's toy
                    hurler-twirler whirled on a string.

Thighs of a gazelle, cannons of an ostrich.
He trots like a wolf, runs like a young fox.
Deep in the heart-girth; the gap between his gaskins
filled to overflow,
and no bone below them askew.
Smooth across the spine as a bride's new griddlestone,
solid as a mill-slab in the ribs.
Blood of big game at his throatlatch—a stain
like tincture of henna combed into an old man's beard.

We sighted a herd, and the cows were like the white-robed
vestals walking circles round the altar-stone.
They turned,
they flew like beads from a breaking necklace,
necklace off a neck
whose father's and mother's
                    brothers sit high in the tribe.
We rode down on the fastest;
                    the rest
of the herd ran hard together, far in his dust.
And he leaped between lead bull and cow
without breaking a lather.

That day, in sum, there was meat on the fire—

some hung high to cure, some turned
at once to steak and stew.

Sunset breeze, and the eye seemed
almost insufficient to sustain
examination of him, looking him hoof to poll.
He stood saddled and bridled,
close in my gaze, the night through.

     Look NOW at the lightning,
     I show you its glitter,
     flutter of light as of brandished hands
     flashing in the piled cloud.
     The stormlight leaps
     like a penitent's lamps
     when he tips oil to the twisted wicks.

I waited the storm with companions
some distance from Darij, a ways from Othaib,
far off my hope's focus.
Thunderhead swirled
              southward over Qatan,
ran to leeward as far
              as Sitar and Yathbul,
and the water began to come down...
Dumped the tamarisks on their whiskers at Kutaifa,
ran the mountain goats out of their lairs
              on the slopes of Qanân,

and left not a palm stump at Taima,
nor any fortification

                or barricade, save those
made out of boulders.

Mount Thabeer, in the thickets of rain,
loomed like a greybeard bundled in his robes.
And at dawn the summit of Mujaimir rose
out of skeins of stormwrack
like a spindle-cap.
And the storm laid out its wares on the desert plain
like a Yemeni unpacking his latest load.

And it seemed, in the early light,
that the valley larks gathered over
nectar laced with nutmeg,
and the carcasses of cougar
drowned down the canyon overnight,
far out in the eye's gaze,
were uprooted onion.

Notations:

The Sophocles doesn't derive from Heidegger's reading of the passage, but neither does it seem to me to replace Heidegger's reading. (Similarly, Morrison's drawing of Poseidon in his Armor isn't, so far as I know, based on Leonardo's Neptune with his Horses; but the two can be looked at together nevertheless to achieve a degree of stereoscopy.)

The Vidyakara poems arise from D.H.H. Ingalls' English versions, not from contact with originals.

This version of the Macuilxochitzin Icuic owes virtually everything, of course, to Miguel León-Portilla's Spanish rendering.

Mohammed Bakir Alwan's immense scholarship is concealed in the Ode.